My Garden Grows

by Frankie Hartley
illustrated by Margeaux Lucas

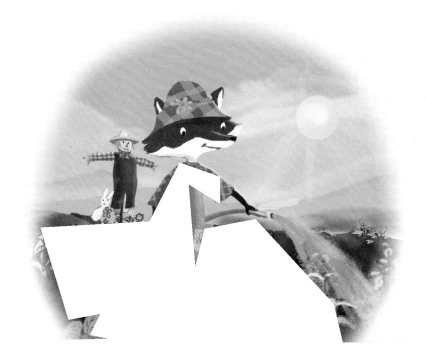

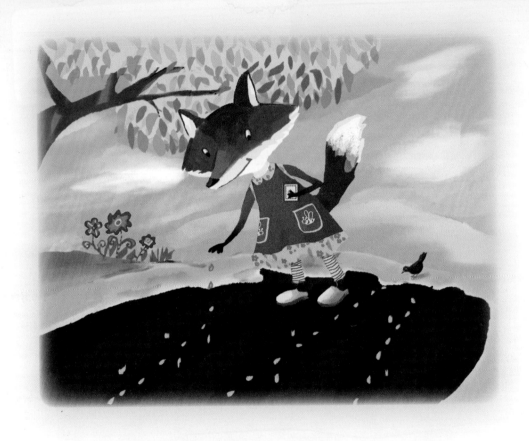

My garden has seeds.

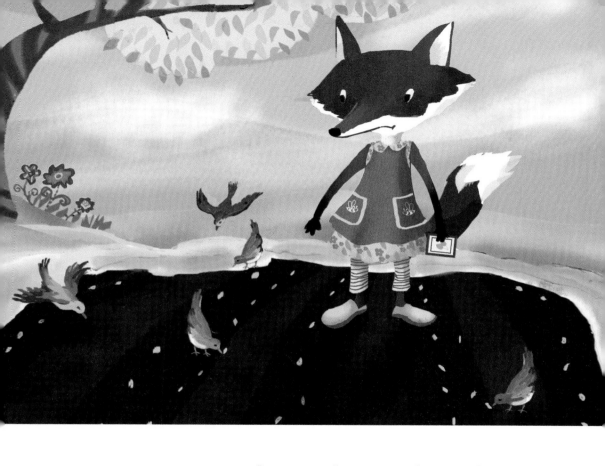

My garden has birds.

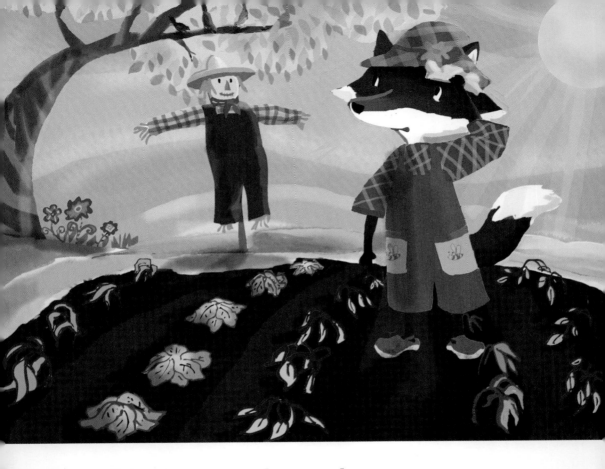

My garden has sun.

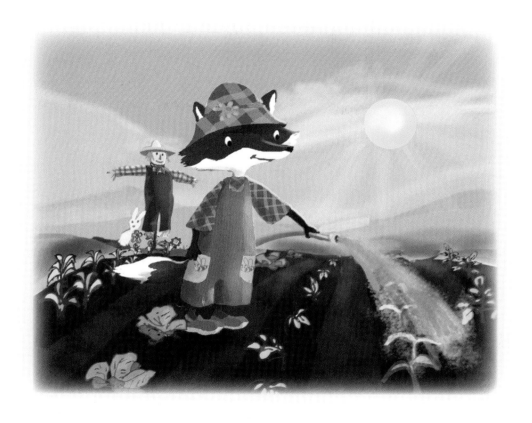

My garden has water.

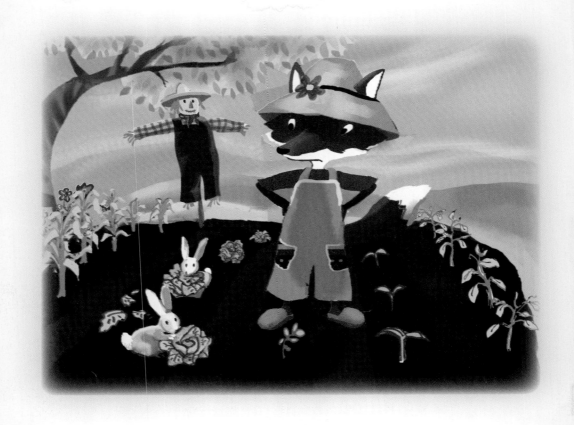

My garden has rabbits.

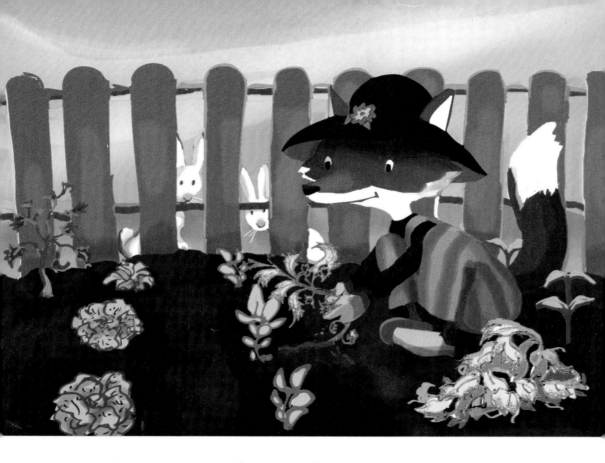

My garden has weeds.

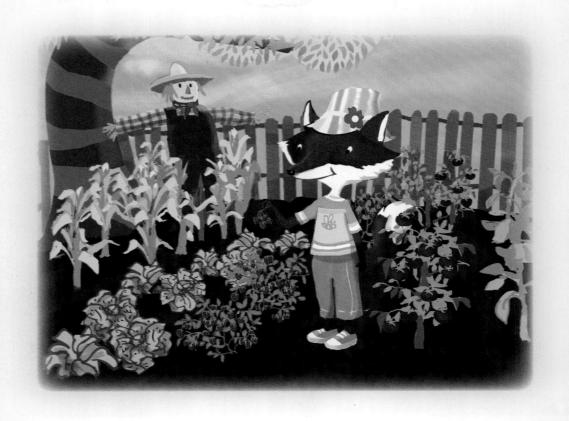

My garden has berries.